Ready To Read

By Lillian Lieberman, James Morrow,
Murray Suid
Illustrated by Corbin Hillam

Publisher: Roberta Suid
Editor: Elizabeth Russell
Cover Design: David Hale
Design and Production: Susan Pinkerton
Cover Art: Corbin Hillam

monday morning®

Monday Morning is a registered trademark
of Monday Morning Books, Inc.

ISBN 0-912107-52-9

Printed in the United States of America

9 8 7 6 5 4 3 2 1

INTRODUCTION

The *Tab and Lil* reading books are high-interest preprimers and primers based on sight vocabulary words. The picture-story theme relates the adventures of Tab and Lil, who play host to Og, a whimsical being from outer space.

Each book contains six stories accompanied by worksheets. The worksheets in each book emphasize different skills and concepts needed in learning to read. Some stories are open-ended for the child to complete creatively by drawing or writing original dialogue.

BOOK I: READY TO READ emphasizes readiness skills and concepts including directional orientation, size, colors, shapes, closure, visual discrimination, consonants, rhyming, and sequencing.

BOOK II: START TO READ emphasizes reading skills. Activities include word discrimination and recognition, phrase and sentence reading and comprehension, rhyming, cause and effect and simple inference skills, following directions, story sequencing, reading mini-stories, and answering simple questions.

BOOK III: READ AND WRITE emphasizes reading and writing skills, including copying and writing words and simple phrases, and writing original dialogue for stories.

Other skills practiced in worksheet activities are cutting and pasting, matching, coloring, drawing, circling, and copying.

Sight words are repeated throughout the three readers and in the worksheets. Phonetic words are added to balance the program. Content words help to carry out the story line. The picture sequences aid in associating meaning with the words and give clues to the words themselves.

The imaginative content of the readers motivates and stimulates the beginning reader to learn the basic words necessary for success in more formal reading instruction. Special Education and English as a Second Language classes may benefit from using these books.

An alphabetical listing of the words used in the books is included for student reference. This list was compiled from the Dolch List, a list of 220 high-frequency prereading sight vocabulary words.

General Directions

INTRODUCE the *Tab and Lil* books by presenting the words necessary before each story sequence. Write the words on the chalkboard or on large cards. Discuss elements of the words to help children learn them, for example, consonants, vowels, rhyming endings, and configuration. Have the children use the words and phrases meaningfully in oral sentences, games, or directions. Make short teacher-class cooperative story charts with the vocabulary words that the children can refer to. Have the children make and illustrate their own stories to share with the class or parents.

MOTIVATE the reading of the stories by telling the children that they are going to meet three characters who have some interesting adventures. Their many adventures are told in picture sequences and simple sentences. Aid the reading and discussion by asking questions such as:

— What are the characters doing? Who are they? What are they like?
— What are they saying? Why? Where do they live? How do they feel?
— What is happening? Why is it happening? What will happen next?
— What other details do you notice? How would you change or end the stories?
— What do you think might happen in the next episode?

EXTEND the readers with the worksheets to give more practice and reinforcement for sight vocabulary, simple phonics and phonetic analysis, simple concept development, comprehension, and writing skills.

ENCOURAGE and help the children to read and follow the directions on each page. The simple exercises are designed to give added support to learn words presented in the stories and to practice other readiness and reading skills.

Encourage children to use the story content and words to aid them in drawing conclusions and in writing their own endings.

ENJOY creative play using these different adventures of Tab, Lil, and Og. Children can draw or make up their own funny incidents and act them out. Such activities will create on-going motivation and interest for the adventures of Tab, Lil, and Og.

After completing the stories, children can take them home to share and practice their new skills.

"Ready to Read" Skills List

Readiness Skills:

- Recognition and discrimination of:
  - shapes: circle, square, rectangle, triangle, oval
  - patterns
  - colors: yellow, green, brown, red, blue, black
- Concepts:
  - size: big, little
  - directions: up, down
- Sequencing:
  - picture sequences
  - letter sequences in words
  - word sequence in phrases and sentences
- Closure:
  - pictures
  - letters and words to be traced
- Visual discrimination:
  - attention to picture details
  - letters of the alphabet
  - words
- Sight word reinforcement
- Fine motor skills:
  - tracing lines, objects, letters, words
  - copying letters, words, figures

Word Identification Skills:

- Clues:
  - pictures
  - word forms
  - meanings
  - letters
- Phonetic analysis:
  - rhyme elements
  - final consonants
  - sound-symbol association

Comprehension Skills:

- Literal meaning:
  - identifying details — who, what
  - word-picture associations (relationships)
  - following directions
  - sequence of events
  - naming objects, characters in pictures
  - supplying missing word in context
- Interpreting:
  - interpreting pictures and picture sequences
  - anticipating and predicting outcomes
  - drawing conclusions
  - identifying what is missing or wrong
  - making inferences using picture clues
  - interpreting word, phrase, sentence meaning

WORD LIST

a
all
am
and
at

ball
bat
big
bike
bird
black
blue
brown

can
cat
cloud
come

Dad
dog
down
draw

end

fun

get
go
good
green

hat
here
him
hit

I
in
is
it

let
let's
like
Lil
little
look

make
Mom

no

Og
on

pet
play
pool

rain
red

see
ship
stay
sun

Tab
that
the
them
this

up

wall
was
we
wet
what
who

yellow
yes
you

Puppet Patterns

Tab and Lil

Here it is!

It is a big ship.

He is little.

Name________________________________

Name

Draw the missing part.

Name

Match. Draw a line.

Name________________________________

Color the things that are up.

Name________________________________

Color the things that are big.

Name

Cut and paste in order.

1.	2.	3.

Name ______________________________

Match the words. Draw a line.

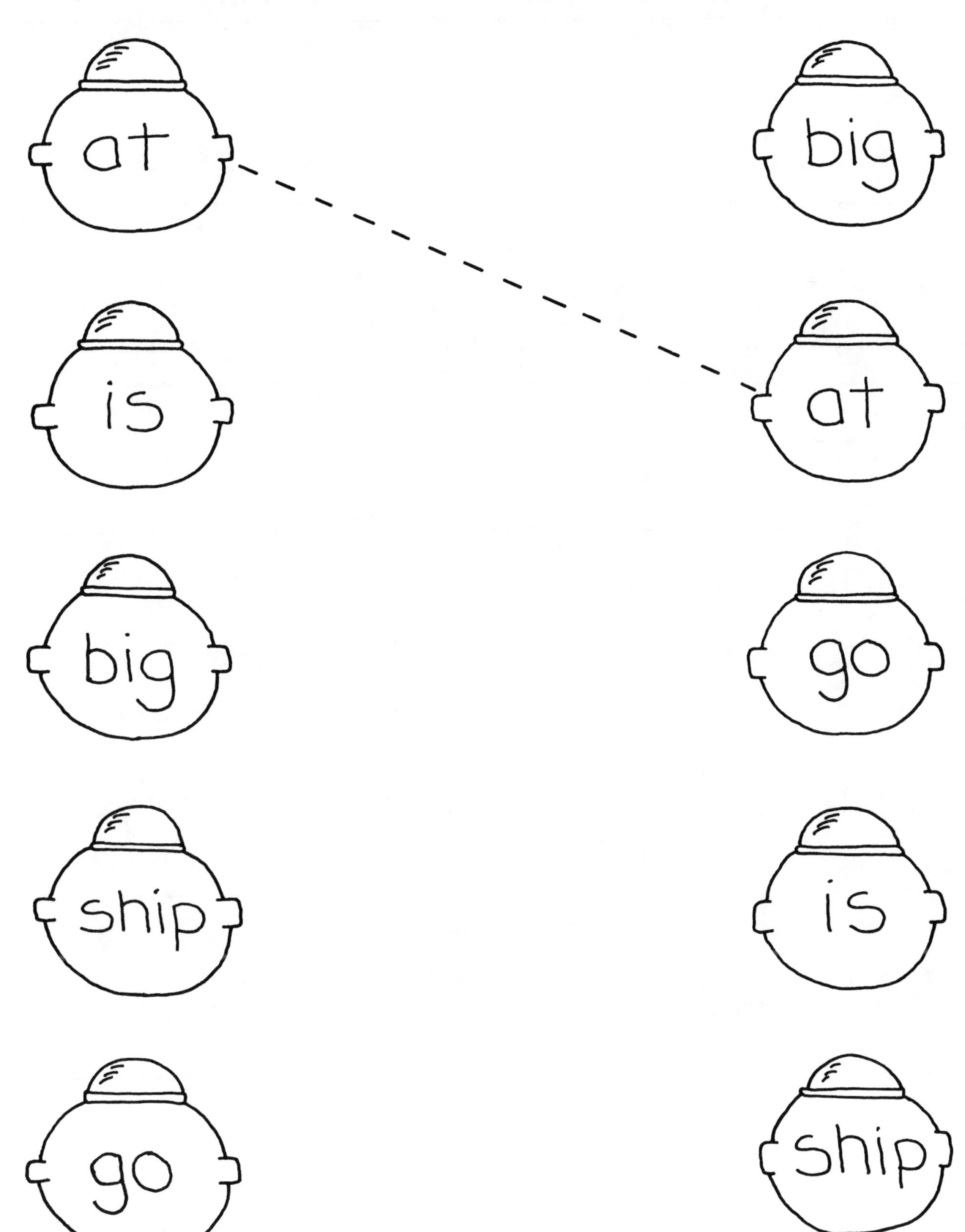

Name______________________________

Read	Trace	Write
look	look	
come	come	
go	go	

Ring the words that are the same.

look	like	look	look
come	come	cat	come
go	on	go	go

Og

I am Lil.

Who are you?

I am Og.

Come see
Mom and Dad.

Name________________________________

Name ________________________________

Color the shapes that are the same.

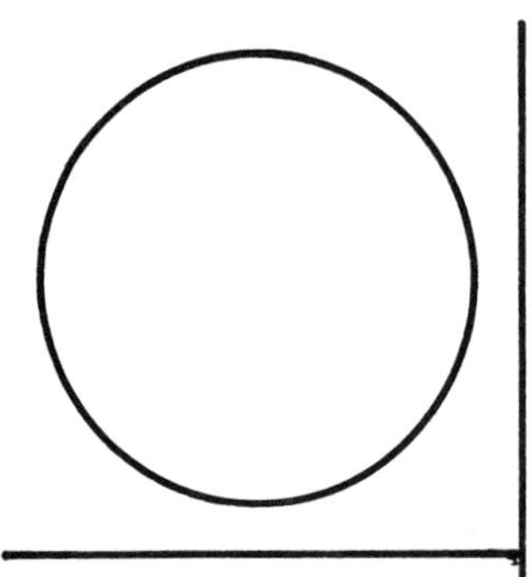
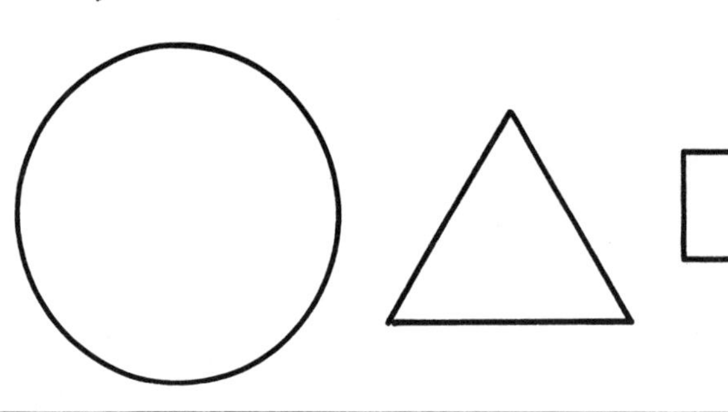
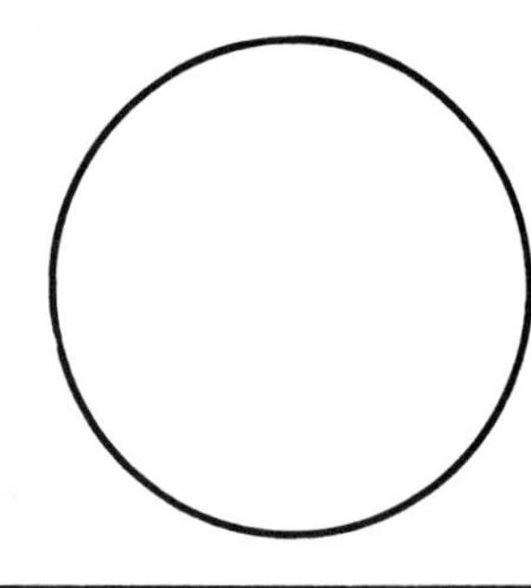

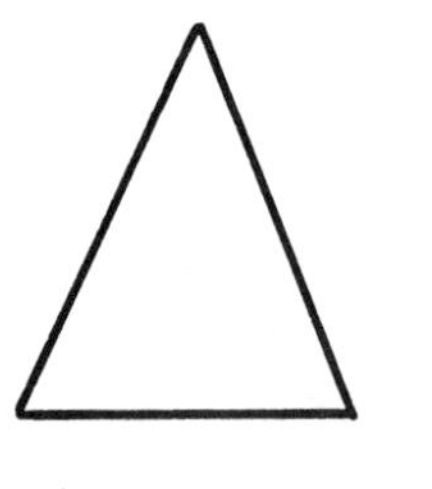

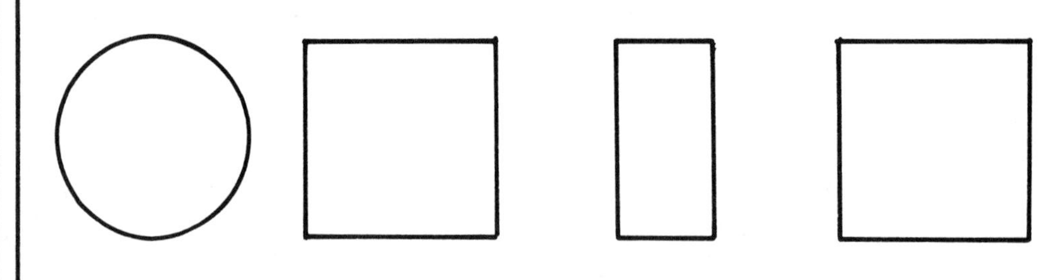

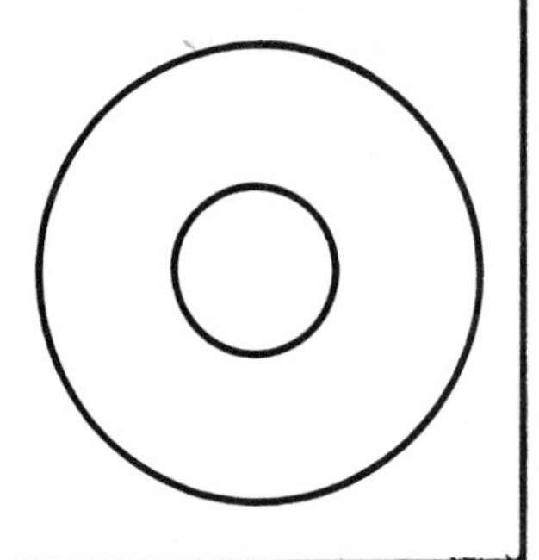
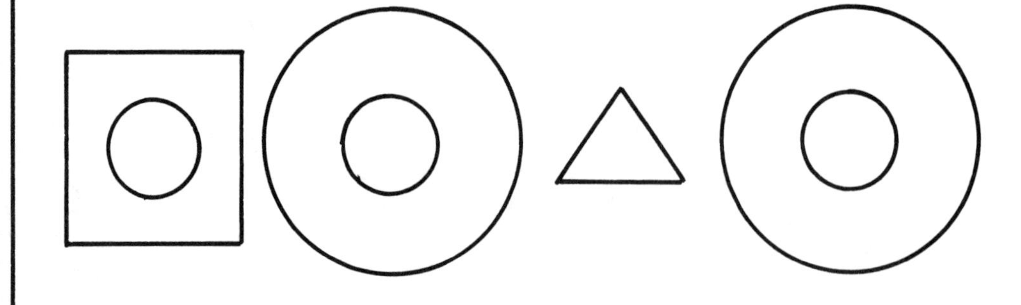

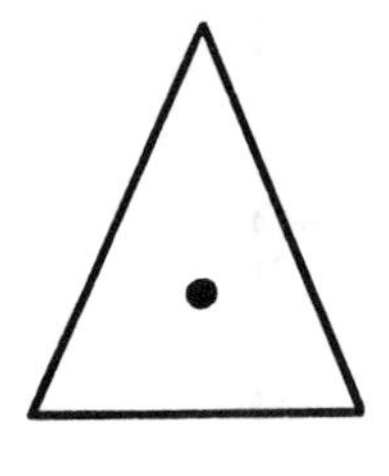
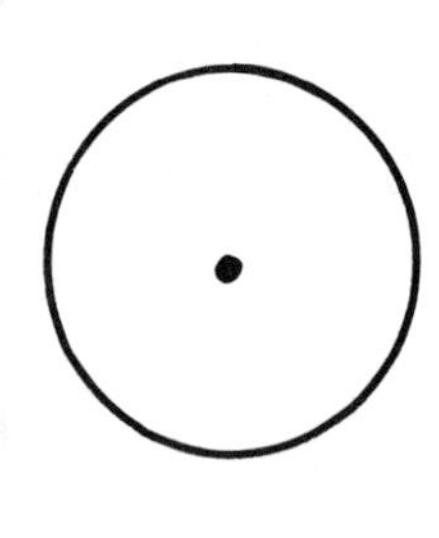

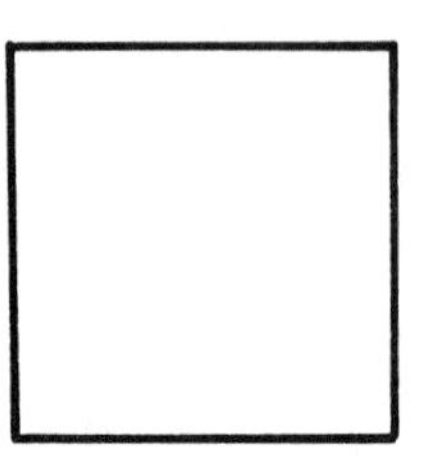
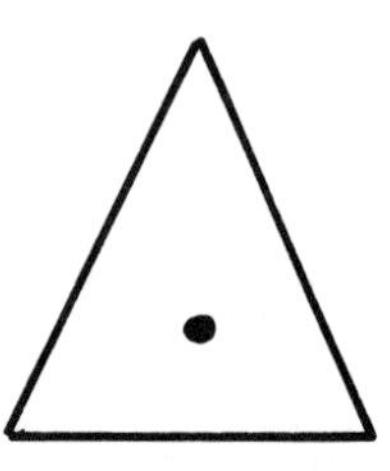

Name ____________________

Draw a picture of you.

Name

Cut and paste. Match.

I am Og.

I am Lil.

I am Tab.

Name____

Color ○ green . Color □ red .

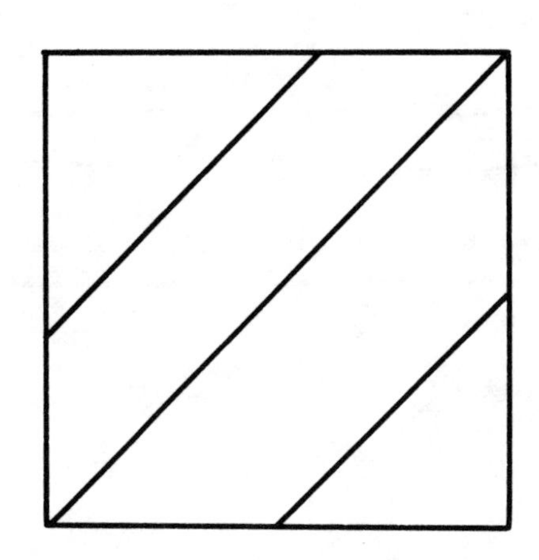

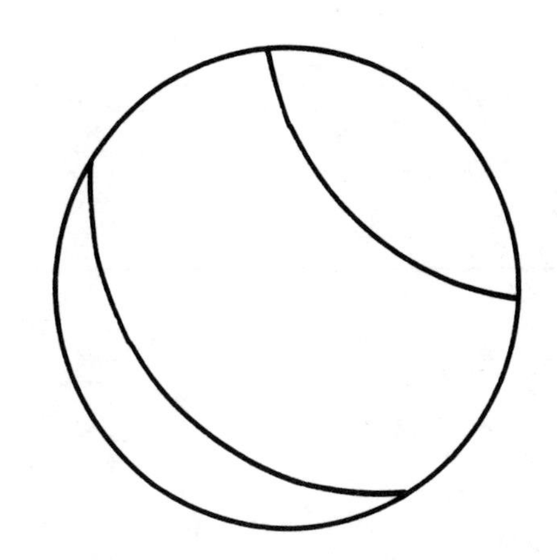

Name____

Color the pictures that are the same.

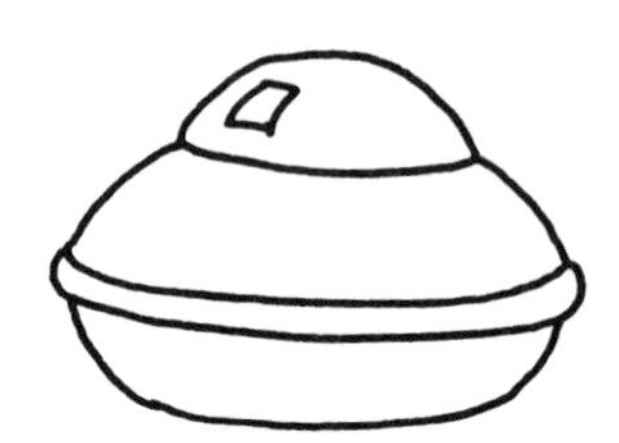
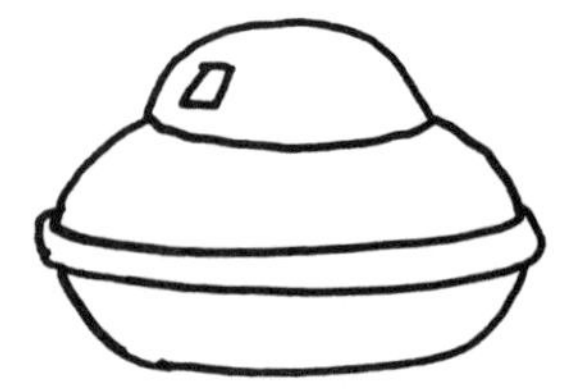

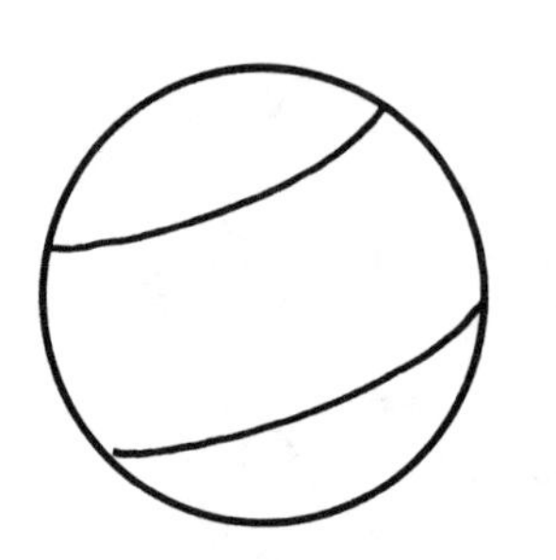
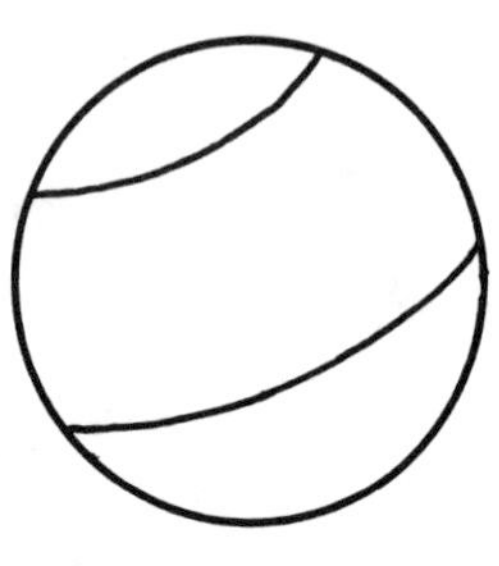

Name________________________________

Color the things that are down.

Name

Read	Trace	Write
you	you	
who	who	
are	are	

Ring the words that are the same.

you	you	yes	you
who	how	who	who
are	are	am	are

Mom and Dad

That was fun!

Here are Mom and Dad.
This is Og.

Can Og stay and play?
Yes!

Come on!

What is that, Lil?

That is a bird.

Can I get on it?
No, Og.

Name____

Color ○ green △ blue.

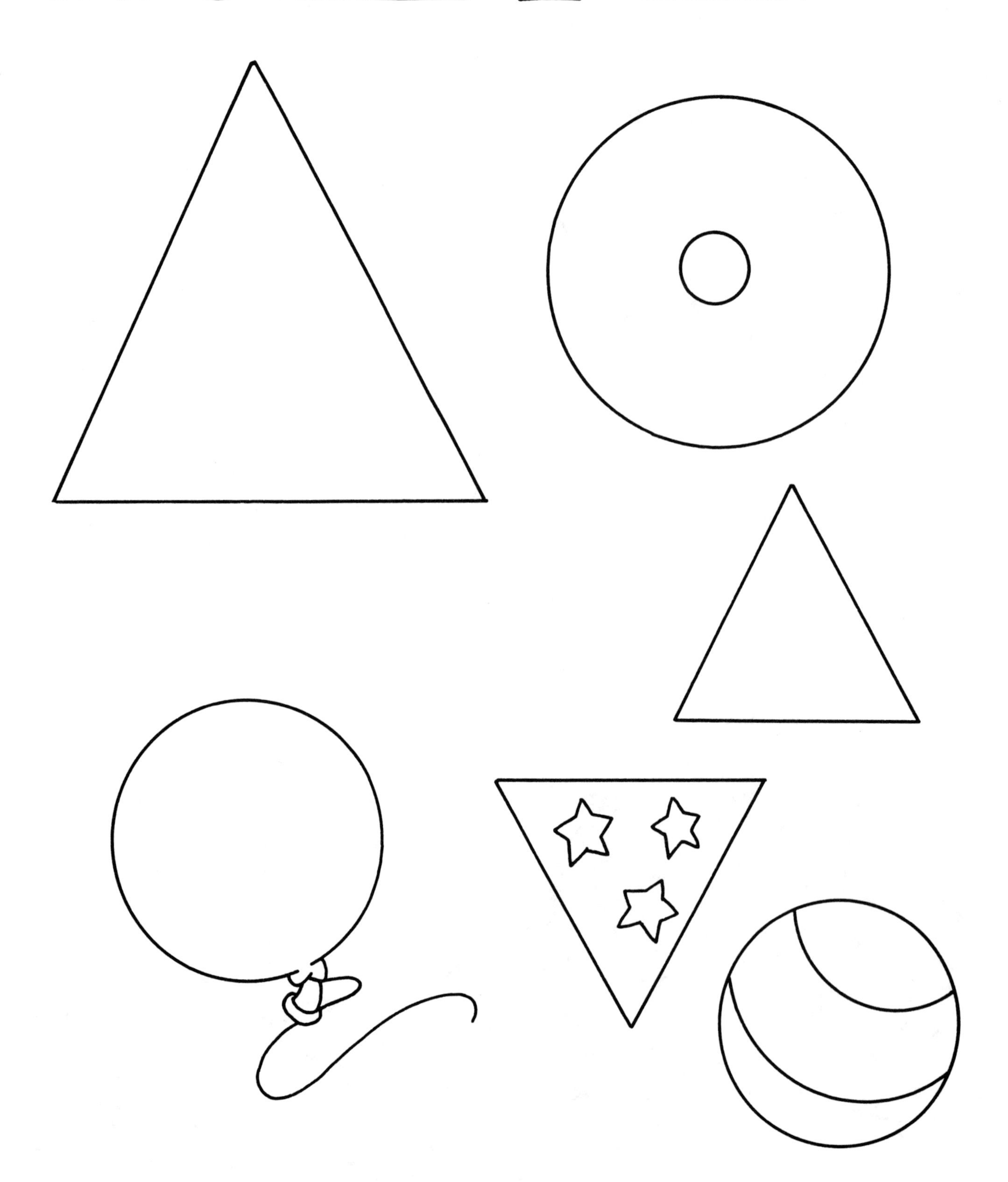

Name________________________________

Write the first letter.

___an

___at

___an

___og

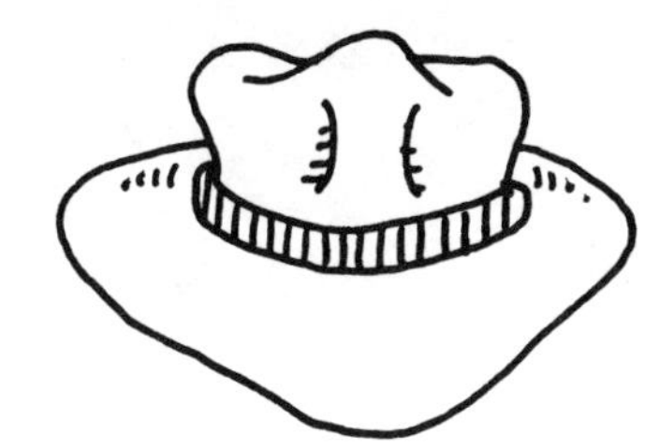

___at

Name______________________________

Match. Draw a line.

Mom

bike

can

Lil

Dad

Og

Tab

Name____

What is first? Cut and paste.

1.

2.

1.

2.

Name

Ring the letters that are like the first.

b	t	b	d	b
n	m	n	n	r
a	a	c	o	a
t	l	t	k	t
c	o	c	a	c
r	r	n	r	m

Name ______________________________

Match. Draw a line.

come	play
like	get
you	come
it	no
get	like
no	you
play	it

Name

Read	Trace	Write
that	that	
was	was	
a	a	

Ring the words that are the same.

that	that	that	the
was	saw	was	was
a	a	at	a

Og and the Pets

What is this, Tab?

This is a hat, Og.
I like it!

What is that?

That is a cat.

A cat is a pet.

Is that a cat?

No. That is a dog.

Name____

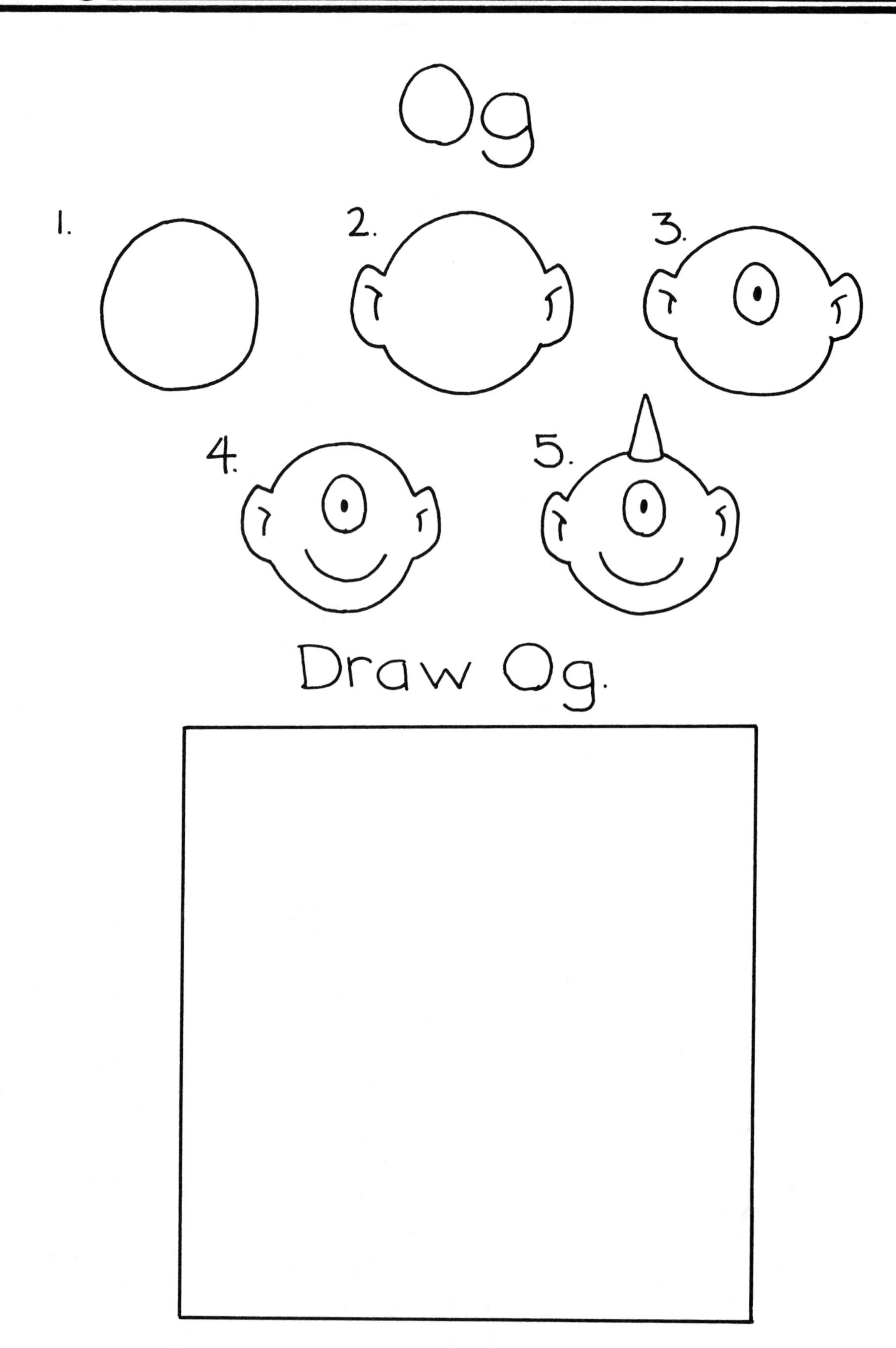

Name________________________________

Color △ ◁ yellow ▯ □ ◁ green ▯.

Name ______________________________

Cut and paste. Name each picture.

What is this?

What is this?

What is this?

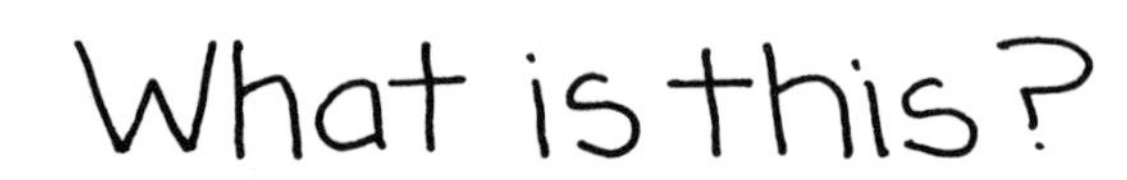

a dog	a cat	a hat	a can

Name________________________________

Cut. Mix. Find 2 cards that are the same.

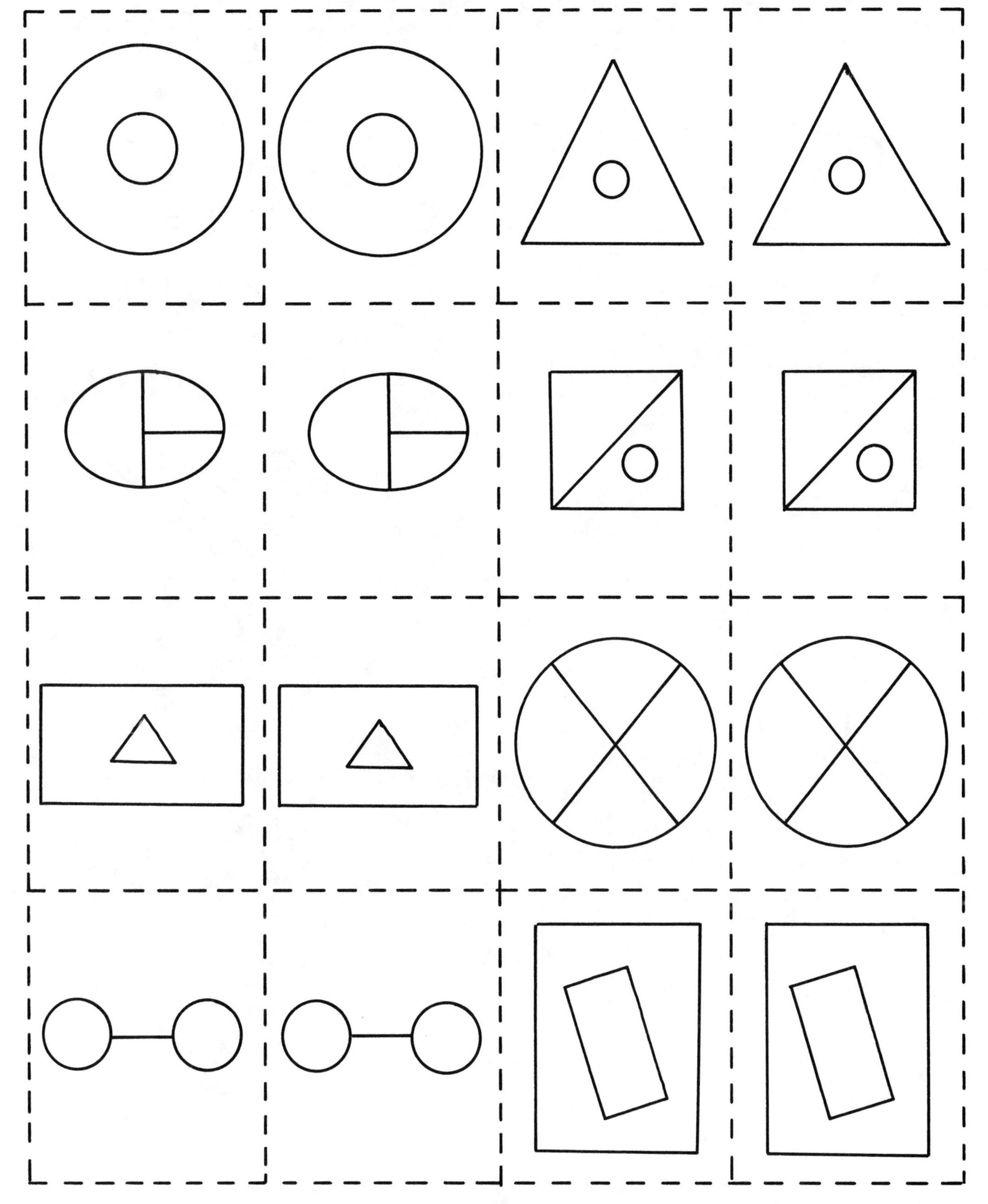

Name ____________________

Match. Draw a line.

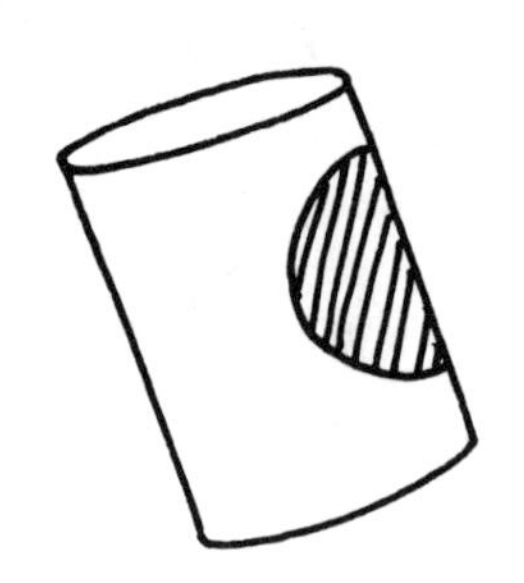

cat

dog

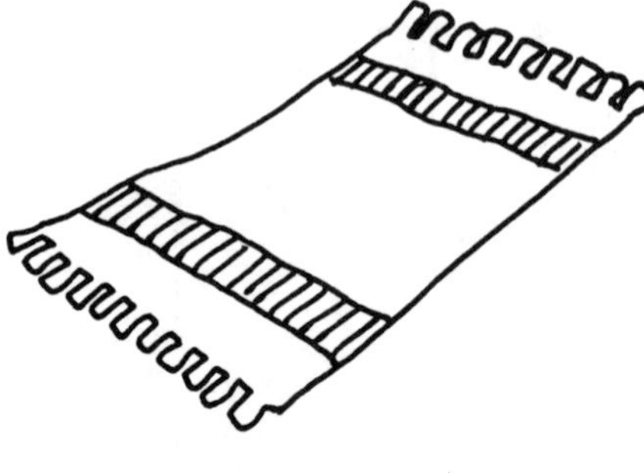

hat

can

bike

mat

Name________________________________

Color the things that rhyme with <u>can</u>.

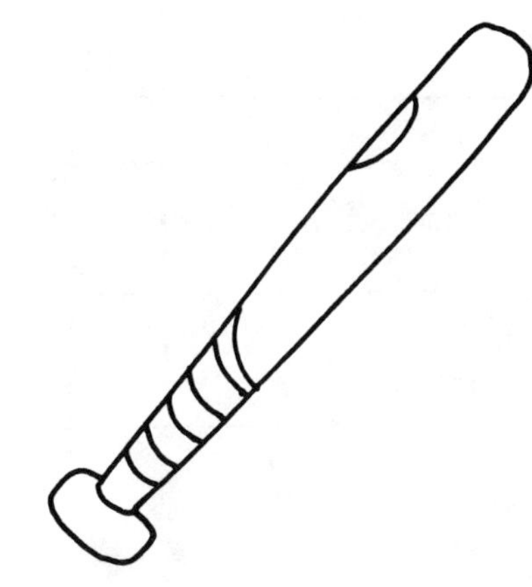

Name

Read	Trace	Write
what	what	
is	is	
this	this	

Read

Draw

This is a hat.

This is a can.

Og on a Wall

See them play.

What is that?

That is a bat.

What is that?

That is a ball.

See him hit the ball!

You can get it, Og.

Name

Color the things that rhyme with bat.

Name ____________________

Match the words. Cut and paste.

wall	that	this	what	ball

Name____

Write the last letter.

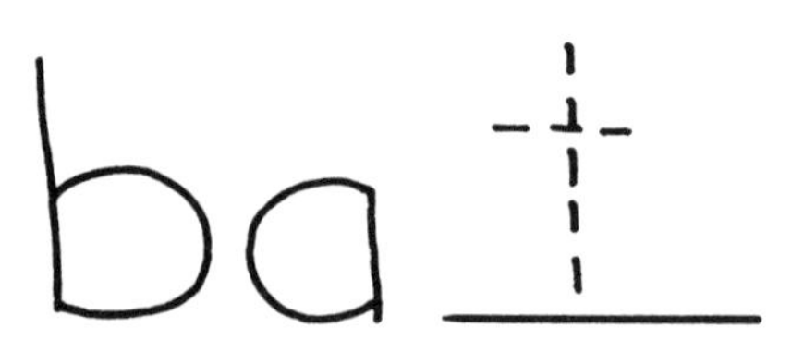

do ___

Li ___

Ta ___

Name ______________________

Write the letter that makes the first sound.

 __an	m c g t
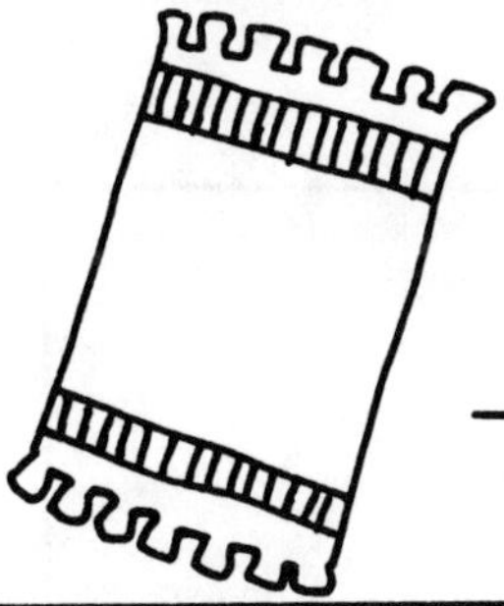 __at	f p m s
 __an	d s c f
 __og	t d m v
 __at	k w h r

Name____

Color ▭ red. Color △ yellow.

Name________________________________

Cut and paste. Match the sentences to the pictures.

This is a cat.

This is a big hat.

This is hot.

This is a bat.

Name

Read	Trace	Write
see	see	
get	get	
him	him	

Ring the words that are the same.

see	sun	see	sit	see
get	get	go	get	got
him	hem	him	hot	him

Og Gets Wet

That is the sun.

You draw it.

This is fun!

I can make rain.

We are all wet.

Name____

Color the ⬭ black.

Name

Read	Trace	Write
make	make	
wet	wet	
all	all	

Ring the words that are the same.

make	make	me	make
wet	we	wet	wet
all	all	at	all

Name________________________________

Write the last letter.

l g n d

poo___

rai___

clou___

o___

Name ____________________

Color the words that rhyme with wet.

Name________________________________

Draw a line. Match.

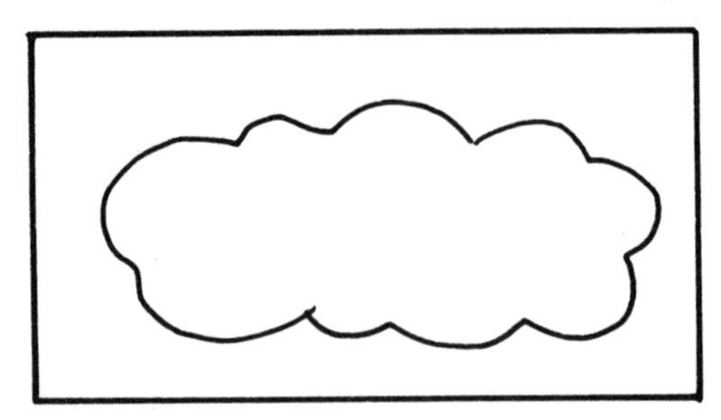

That is rain.

That is the sun.

That is a cloud.

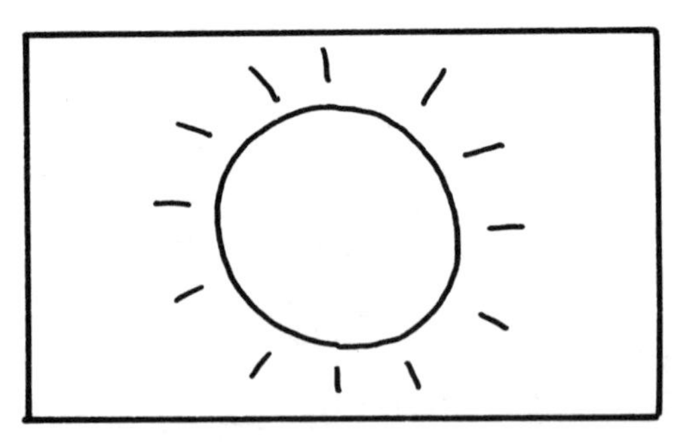

That is a pool.

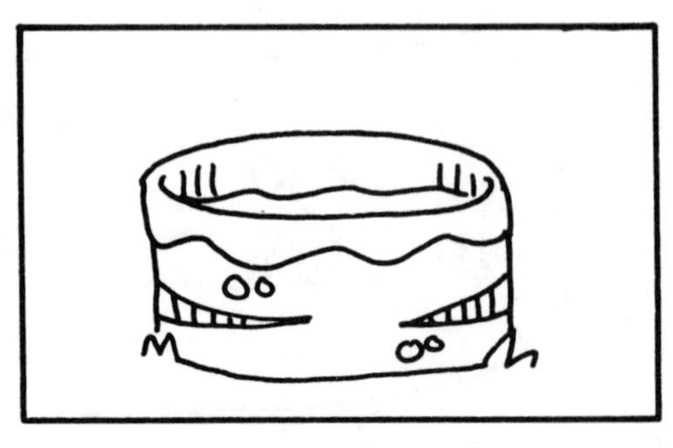

Og is wet.